VOICE
/
POEMS

Voice / Poems
by Susan Azar Porterfield

TRIO
HOUSE
PRESS

Copyright © July 1, 2025 Susan Azar Porterfield

No part of this book may be used or performed without written consent of the author, if living, except for critical articles or reviews.

Azar Porterfield, Susan
1st edition

ISBN: 978-1-949487-46-6
Library of Congress Control Number: 2024951274

Interior design by Natasha Kane
Cover art by Jeffrey Scherer
Cover design by Baonhia Xiong
Editing by Heidi Czerwiec

Trio House Press, Inc.
Minneapolis
www.triohousepress.org

For DeKalb Poets, Ink.
Ubuntu: I am what I am, because of who you all are

Table of Contents

Writing Poems   3

I. A Laughing so Sharp

Archeologists Discover Mummy with Golden Tongue	7
Voice	8
Alternative Facts	9
Today I Left Food Out for a Feral Cat	11
Some Dog is Barking	12
All God's Creatures	13
The Problem with Staying Level	14
Last Morph: Tree to Woman	16
A Thing or Two about Illness	17
Irritable, after Fact and Reason	18
Death of a Nine-Month-Old Girl, Not My Own	19
Once Out of Nature	20
Over	21
J.M.W. Turner, *Slavers Throwing overboard the Dead and Dying—Typhoon coming on*	22

II. Don't Be Afraid

House Poems

Dreamed Room	25
The House Teaches Her About Death	26
The House Becomes Strange	27
The House Teaches Her About Love	28
Still of the Tongue	29
The House Falls and Rises, Rises and Falls	30
The House is Not a Womb	32
A House Once Experienced	33
Story of a Little Time	34
My Sister and I Tease Each Other Over Which of Us Will Be More Wrecked by the Death of Our Spouses	35
Girls at Play Learn that Exquisite the Body	36
Angel from Montgomery	37

III. I Shall Go Into a Hare

Soul & Self Walk Into a Bar

Self 101, Soul 101	41
Soul & Self	42
This is Just	43
Soul Needs Its Space	44
What Self Learns from Soul	45
What Soul Learns from Self	46
The Real Deal	47
Soul Wants	48
Big Bang Genesis	49
The Hot, New Indignation	50
Soul & Self GPS	51
Heisenbergian Humor	52
Soul & Self on Tour	53
Who's on First?	54
The Value of the Liberal Arts	55
Self 301, Soul 301	56

IV. Wander Window

Still Life, Nocturne in Shimmer and Bird	59
Ubiquitous Porosities	60
Story	61
Frost, Midnight, the Burbs	62
Sometimes the World Makes Itself Known to You	63
From a Perception of Only 3 Senses or 3 Elements None Could Deduce a Fourth or Fifth	64
I Don't Know What I Mean by this Poem, but I Know It's True	65
Those We Love	66
Scientists Find New Organs in the Center of the Head	67
Clean the Glass, Open the Window	68
Kind of Thing that Happens When Nothing Happens	69
Andromeda Galaxy in Ultraviolet	70
The Road was a Ribbon of Moonlight	71
Acknowledgments	73

Writing Poems

Wherever there will be nothing, read that I love you
Diderot, Letter to Sophie Volland, 1759
    —Derrida, *Memoirs of the Blind*

Maybe you've idled on a country road at night,
you in the car alone, farmer's fields on either side,

and because you needed, right then, to be kissed,
you flipped off the lights and hit the gas,

the road before you a blank paper sheet,
lacking line or lip, as if you were writing

in the emptied dark without being able to see.

I.
A Laughing so Sharp

Archeologists Discover Mummy with Golden Tongue

The tongues ... were probably meant to help the deceased
speak in the afterlife, experts said.
　　　　—New York Times

Glossa of gold foil/Ace up your sleeve.

Once you get there, where you're going,

you'll have to make your case.

In Christian-town, you're de facto in or out.

Tongue of dust. Nothing much anyway

to say. No

　　　　honey words daubed on the darling's nipples.

Licked sticky off lips. Words

spun from filigreed threads, *whisper thin,*

warm-moisting an ear.

　　　　　　　Hear me out, wait.

What I think I meant. After all, after all,

will I be saved?

Voice

I shall go into a hare,
—Isobel Gowdie, 1662, Self-Identifying Witch

Pressed against the ragged seam of sleep,
I've heard voices.

Don't be afraid, warm-breathed
in my ear. *Wander window* was told, was told,

and one time, strangely,
I shall go into a hare.

"Your imagination," soothed my parents
early on, and that seemed right,

as if a sparrow had nested in my chest,
something intimate, something odd.

And only once did I hear a laughing so sharp
it bit the inside of my mouth.

Alternative Facts

A bomb has been tossed
in the middle of this poem,

well, let's not say *middle*.
Try *first encountered heart*, i.e.,

a pivot centered round
mostly equal parts about a start,

and by *start*
I actually mean/I don't mean

beginning, though you
might think so.

That's up to you.
I may mean *astonish*, maybe

flush out, as in rabbits or deer,
(better to keep things loose, pensez vous?)

Take *crown of thorns*, e.g. With that
there's blood. Avoid blood.

Also bones, spit, and piss.
Flirt with *crown of twigs* or better,

nature's wreath. Make language your whore.
Clarity kills, as in

"Please, I'm hungry."
"I'm afraid to die."

Statements pure as rushing your body
onto a humming grenade.
Push this meme instead,
He *repositioned his self for maximum effect.*

Today I Left Food Out for a Feral Cat

All day long, I clean house the way lovers, at last,
undress. The world lightens and lightens. Global
peace seems sure. Thus, I eat an orange.
A dog licks my hand.

When, in the kitchen,
a muffin crumb falls some unknown where,
I get down on my knees to lynx-eye under cupboards,
in places where two seams meet.

If I could, I'd say "sorry" to the boy whose
dime I took from the top of his desk in 1st grade.
It was just there, and I thought I'd found it
but somehow knew to lie when later asked.

Some Dog is Barking

We don't know where.
Behind us? Next block down? The next?
A cut-crystal echo-call that at times
you can forget to hear, the shout or cry,
as if alone, aware-alone, but then,
maybe not, maybe someone will come or hear?

We don't know. We don't know.

And then, sometimes, the barking stops,
and we think, ah, someone has come.
Is the day blue now and sun? Where's water?
Is there a hand like love stroking a head?

But mostly, most often, there's barking.

And even if there's no barking,
at night, in bed, we whisper *Poor thing*,
staring into the dark. *Poor thing*.

All God's Creatures

On second thought, God decided to make humans
in such a way that to them, pigs tasted
like heaven. Cows too.

As well as other miscellaneous beings—
All very random, really. Who wound up in the mouth,
molded to meet the mmm, mmm good, molecular/genetic urge

of God's own making. While others were, you know,
just meh. Sure, God could've gone the other way,
contrived so no one seemed yummy to anybody else,

(Word is, God could do anything God wants.)
but God liked seeing the struggle, human-creatures beating
against the chest of their own God-fashioned natures

because after God had performed the world, there
wasn't much else to do. And being God, God foresaw
that God would get bored, so the suspense kept God's

attention. How would it all turn out? Stay tuned to see if humans
finally grow more angelic. Will they swing that sledge hammer?
Wring that neck? Watch them rationalize torture

to pop some flesh on the grill. Best of all, God
gets to play the free-will card, built right in. What a piece of
work is man. How noble in reason. In apprehension,

yep, how like a god.

The Problem with Staying Level

Before you're going to
fall, you don't know it,

no sexy-apple-
God-damn test.

You're not overreaching, hell no.
You're innocent, I swear, standing

on ground dense as air,
concrete slabs and their promises,

> *We're solid, Baby,*
> *as nothin' is.*

Before you fall,
you can't hear, you can't feel

the constant molecular
deconstructions

blasting beneath your toes
or sense how thin-to-breaking

your assumptions, really,
have always been.

The moment before

you could be touching your face
or writing a poem,

snoring in your tight, little bed,
driving dimly along, believing:

"the very last thing I feel
I'm doing"

is exactly the thing you are doing.

Last Morph: Tree to Woman

Then did she wonder
that blossoming fingers and hair

somehow had failed to attain
as they'd done every spring since she turned.

Bark that long bit her thigh softened
its jaw, and her heart in the heart

of the laurel green, rhyming itself to breath,
opened a door once latched.

Could she then go?

Already her foot, slipping free,
touched earth, and hunger resharpened her tongue.

Already the bluntness of literal space
her reaching hand grasped let her know

she would be, from now on, female:
female only, female as any bitch, as any sow.

A Thing or Two About Illness

Probably you think when you cough up blood, if you've never coughed up blood, that you'll be all hysterical and crying and gasping, but no, you just stare into the scarleted tissue and think, Oh, I see, because you don't feel that bad, maybe a bit run down, maybe losing a little weight, not sleeping well, but otherwise, you know, okay, so this rosy text comes out of the blue, like a break-up note when you'd been planning a sexy jaunt to the Keys, and you read it again and again, to get the tone just right, the darker, maroonish jots amid pink swirling, and you sit in the shadow of your room, in your bed, holding the napkin like a blossom in your open palm, and turn, blinking, to look out the lace-curtained window at the night's grey, the maple branches, indifferent black, a quiet, waiting hum, and at last you think, I should tell the husband, still up in the next room, and you bring him the cloth, and he thinks, Oh, I see, and both of you decide it's late, though you're still spluttering red. You'll phone in the morning. And you conspire. You conspire. To forget in your terrible love.

Irritable, After Fact and Reason

For Andee

Reaching again.
Grief, I've been told, is that.

Because you wanted to go,
I shadowed, just in case, so when,

in my dream,
you began to puke, bent over,

I could hold you up,
away from the muck, your party dress

untouched, mostly. And mine too
or, at least, nothing that couldn't be

unsoiled.
In Paris, that one time, you'd tripped,

sprained your wrist. In the ER
at the Hôtel-Dieu, *Everyone falls in the street*,

the doctor said, then smiled,
Ce n'est pas un strip-tease,

when your blouse silked away.
I'd never seen such a beautiful bosom as yours.

I want you to know that.

But yeah, here I am, absurd,
asking the impossible again.

Death of a Nine-Month-Old Girl, Not My Own

How to enter.
A hook to hang *why*. As if, *I'm home*,
time for tea. And so, *home*.
As if.

Start again.

How to enter the open door,
door being always open. No
inner no out.

Who lied? Who said *fair*?

Who, in god's name, said *soul*?

There's a father so in love,
he's not afraid to die.

Starlings, darlings,
                      children of stars?

each in the flock connected, adjusting
a wing's bite of air
                      as the wing of the neighbor
adjusts

and then again   and then again

the swoop rises, the swoop twists, it falls,
rises
            rises.

Once Out of Nature

You have one job. Oh body, oh my God, we
are a glory, tiny veins in our fingers,
pulley of skin working index and thumb.
*

They try to steal the baby, the females,
sidling up, sniffing. If the mother
is distracted, another chimp, touching
the baby's leg may gently pull
the warm, curious weight away
to clutch in her own encircling arms.
*

When I sleep in winter,
I'm like a curled-up fist. I long
for the yellow of butter and bread.
*

Raining hard. A man carrying groceries
and a child asked could I hold her
as he ran to unlock his car. She was
a little radish in the earth. Her body,
snug as a nest.
*

Even in March, there's some unclenching,
though we've all been hurt before. Still,
a scratching, scratching is heard,
or maybe it's an itch?
*

When the funeral ends, we head to the buffet.
The wife of sixty years fixes herself a plate.
*

My sister lives in Miami, her son in L.A.
He has children of his own. There was a time
I needed something like that, my body starving
as if, without, it would break in two.
Which seems odd when I think about it now.

Over

Late October--what happens
next?

The earth moving re-moves my
focus,

each moment inviting the then and
then:

Petunias nag me for drink.
I'm deaf to their pleas.

Milk on the verge spilled now
(why wait?).

Novels I won't read twice.
Return texts I just won't send.

                    You say,
fusty peaches may revive as pie,

but, confess it, Luv, rebirth's rare.
Let's err on the possible's side,

clean desk, new book, April
seedlings swaddled in their beds.

      You know.

You know how this will end,
how it starts.

And.

J.M.W. Turner, *Slavers Throwing overboard the Dead and Dying—Typhoon coming on*

The leg is delicate enough to be female, chained
by an iron anklet

                *

cut free   under the roiling, still alive
yet alive we guess

                *

that small, seen foot thrills sharp
as a dancer's, tense with blood   terror's
what's wanted

                *

       purple/blue storm-light, storm-clouds
against whose chest we beat,

                *

carried off, cut loose, tossed out—

                *

the guilty ship struggles to write
its story too   already a ghost.

II.
Don't Be Afraid

House Poems

Dreamed Room

There are rooms you are returned to
that you've never been in before.

You are re-minded,
oh yes, *oh yes:*

bright windows, floor to ceiling,
and doors unleashed, unleashing.

The House Teaches Her About Death

After he died, he came to call,
waiting at the basement door

though she couldn't reach it
to let him cross in

what with the party, people cocktailing,
and when she looked again,

he was gone.

Frantic, she leapt up the stairs,
yanked open the door, and saw him, yes,

the line of his back, his walk.
She could see him still,

waiting to cross at a light, crossing,
stopping to adjust the strap of his pack.

I can reach him, she thought, running now.
I can make it just in time.

The House Becomes Strange

Waking as usual, she began to doubt her hands
were her hands, and certainly

these arms, which refused to reach for her glasses
on the stand where she'd left them,

did not belong to her.
To stretch and grasp took oh, so long. It annoyed her,

the slow plow of body through waves of air,
and now, standing upright at last, she couldn't

find the silly bathroom, which was not
where it was supposed to be.

The whole structure had shaken loose . . .
lightness became her, and from its own knock,

her heart, huddled in its little lived-space,
silently shied away.

The House Teaches Her about Love

They seemed a stream of need flowing by her legs,
five or six of them, seven, she wasn't sure, children,

young, vague, but the house would help her
keep them alive. It was large and light--

here, we're safe, she sighed,

meaning absence, mainly, from vigilance,
the mind twisting, cat-eared, to clicks and creaks,

snap-deciding now again now
about which sounds not to fear.

She ran to secure each window and door,
all locked, all tight.
                    Except that one.

Fumbling with the latch
she saw outside a darkness outlined in dark--

and now she had to get them out out, quick,
away from the house that, dammit, wasn't hers anyway

just shelter she'd found by chance, and those kids
weren't hers either, you know.

Still of the Tongue

Words slam shut in her face,
right as she's set to sail through,

just as a hip or eye can crash for no reason, no
reason, so language, long

red-carpeting her path, crumples up,
trips her tongue.

    I say for the first time

again, "No, no, it's a gift," the third time
she asks what she owes, what she owes,

what she owes, latches fated
open/closed, she softly slipping

like light, like air . . . .

I never know what room holds her,
what echo she's shadowed down what vague hall,

whisperings she can almost make out,
faint as a turned key's rasp,

the ghost of someone familiar, someone
she might once have known?

The House Falls and Rises, Rises and Falls

Things fall because they are trying to reach their natural place in contact with the earth.
      —Aristotle

Houses fall, sink into earth
and rise slowly, years and years

ripe as plums aching,
top floors gaining, collapsing

on the lower, until all pull up
a quilt of dust

      and then a quiet
and then a rustling and then a

rising, climbing one dim inch,
another, to whatever height

destined the house,
whatever height destined

the crumble,
      and then, who knows why,

a nail pushes off, boards ruffle,
beams creak, and weedy

become walls and floors.
Then,

like a factory-worker clocking
free,

the house rushes now
faster and faster

anxious to be headed
to where it once began.

The House is Not a Womb

Waiting, in the half-dark of our house. In
the half-dark. Waiting, keys in hand.

Some people before me have waited here.
There will be others. I don't know them.

Walls and windows, roof and doors,
they're not pregnant with our presence,

year after year, careening, corner to corner,
 laughter/anger, love/fear.

I see that now.

The house has no heart that contains our heart.
It doesn't nurture; it's not indifferent.

I've no skin, the house has always, always told us
from the moment we swaddled in.

A House Once Experienced

A house that has been experienced is not an inert box
  —Bachelard

The house next door stopped breathing,
and we've become unsure

of how our days keep time. Blind
windows flatten at night, the mute

masquerades as quiet. Empty of
its signal lights flashing who's up,

who's out, their baby's crying
above soft murmurs,

air-borne laughter alighting
on wide-open summer days,

the boy's basement drumming
we learned to love . . .

as if our two structures shared
a way to know human space.

Drifting in patterns, like dreams that follow
each on each night-long, without

the pulse of that house, its rounds,
we begin, as with any passing,

to redraw yet again that same edge:
inside/out, other/us.

Story of a Little Time

They thought she'd died
        but maybe not.

After all, there she was
        sitting across from him as always,

chatting at the breakfast table,
        reading the *Daily Mail*.

Meanwhile, birds flew in and
        out as if the house

were conduit or path. They couldn't
        stop them, and anyway,

they liked the razzle-dazzle of wings,
        though she cautioned, in public,

they shouldn't speak to one another
        lest rude people ask

who you talking to?
        and besides, they themselves

didn't know what the story was
        since they were pretty sure she'd died,

though she wasn't acting dead. And
        in truth, they didn't care.

We could exist this way forever, they thought,
        birds and all, winging

round their place, singing airs
        she in her sleep began to hum.

My Sister and I Tease Each Other Over Which of Us Will Be More Wrecked by the Death of Our Spouses

You, I say,
the way you're always scouting a new job
in case the one you've got buys the farm.

Because when anyone you love is sick,
you drink too much gin. Because you & Woodie
have separate bank accounts, as if, yeah sure,

that'il show 'em, the gods, that the body, though
cut in two, still has its own damn legs, so there. Truth is
we've tinned ourselves up,

you and I, clanking about like cans of yellow corn.
Which is why I sometimes rehearse his death
when he's gone for a walk or to the store, imagining

without, no one coming home. A kind of spell,
self-conjuring this sliver of grief, splintered
off from a larger stash, I hoard as a charm.

                              He laughs
when I tell him this as he's sweeping the kitchen floor,
mindful of the summer spiders that in our corners
have made their lives.

Girls at Play Learn That Exquisite the Body

We didn't call it butterfly kisses,
eyelash-by-eyelash scintillation,

just an oddness, like
        tongue-tip to tongue-

tip, if you were brave for the dare:
        Touch tongues!

This unsettling, just what we
        came here for, how a thing

dull as a tongue could be
        alien/alive, we sensing,

body with another body
        annuls between-space,

finger-tracing, like dragonflies pond-skimming,
        the skin on your sister's back,

light-light, almost not touching, but
        yes, touching, the mundane husk, now hub,

holy self, a shivering.
        Years later, reborn as itch.

Angel from Montgomery

The girl in the dorm room next to mine playing her guitar
must've been sitting, like me,
on the top bunk, other side of the wall,
and she was singing, sweet-voiced, *Make me an angel*, and me,

I wasn't singing, I was studying, hunched over, Poly Sci or French,
and then here was longing like a cut,
and I wanted to be of that world, maybe be her, even
though we'd never met. She didn't care

about stuff like guys, I storytold, wasn't into clothes, junk like that--
she was one of those all-natural types, you know the kind,

like her hair was thick as raw silk, and when she washed it,
she just let it air dry, and she was stunning in her bones in an odd,
go-it-alone way, and, though she didn't write poetry,
I bet she read it and knew who Rilke was, and, like me, sort of kept to
    herself,

not being unfriendly, just quiet,

and she was just like that other girl
in my history class, who was also somehow so cool, and our professor,
who was herself youngish and cool, also got that, I sensed,
the way she treated her more like an equal, and once I saw her—the
    girl—

stopped at a light on her motorcycle, not a big one, but still, I mean,
when do you see a girl like that, like she knew who she was, out there in
    traffic like that,
and she wasn't afraid. She wasn't. And we nodded to each other, slightly,
    before she took off.

III.
I Shall Go into a Hare

Soul & Self Walk into a Bar

Self 101

Hey, what's that?
Self asks, looking in a glass.

That's us, you dolt, Soul says.
Don't you know yourself?

Don't you know yourself?
Self apes

and makes a face.

    *

Soul 101

Get rid of those trashy notions,
Soul says. *It's nothing to do
with God.*

Does God have a soul?
                        Soul asks

Everything alive is ensouled, Self says,
so, you tell me.

    *

Soul & Self

Not dialogue, exactly,
more companionable, like Didi & Gogo

Hardy & Laurel bumbling over each other,

which is really hard to do
when you're the same, which they are

Soul and Self, meaning that's that.

    *

This Is Just

*Let's try for pathos
and poignancy*, they say,

and sometimes, they say,
Let us eat this plum.

Turns out

eating a plum's
the most dumb, heartbreaking thing.

*

Soul Needs Its Space

If I dye my hair blonde, Soul says
       Will you know who I am?

Of course, Self scoffs,
My hair's blonde too, you know.

Is it?
Oh, well then, Soul sighs.

Never mind.

    *

What Self Learns from Soul

Mirror-staring,
Self ponders,

Hmmm. I'm not that charming.

Soul agrees, getting naked,
turning this way and that.

Look at me, now, look at me!
This is how it's done.

*

What Soul Learns from Self

Soul is tired of language
and wants only

to lie out at night under stars.
Self goes too

and yells up at sky,
shut up, shut up,

damn Soul.

    *

The Real Deal

When asleep
      Soul & Self

look so doggone cute,
breathing steadily and calm,

innocently sucking a thumb
and dreaming of the face

they had before they were born.

    *

Soul Wants

I'm hungry, Soul whines, as if
Self's purpose is to cater to Soul's every whim.

Here's Lark Ascending, Self offers.
*Breathe it in. How 'bout a bit
of Hopkins or Yeats? Both great picks.*

No thanks, Soul says,
I'll take steak, slightly pink.

*

Big Bang Genesis

I'm thinking of converting to Judaism,
    Self reveals.

Go for it, says Soul, *and me,*
    I'll become Sikh.

What were you before?
    Self asks.

Trailing clouds of glory.

   *

The Hot, New Indignation

Self is outraged,
         and Soul is bored.

Really? This again?

Soul's *ennui* outrages Self,
though in truth

Self is also a tiny bit bored.

This really outrages Soul.

    *

Soul & Self GPS

Self wants Soul to commit
to infinity. Soul wants Self
to commit to the here and now.

For a moment,

when they awaken, they have no idea
where the Hell
they are.

      *

Heisenbergian Humor

Hold still, I'm trying to measure you for posterity, Soul says.

Giggling, Self asks, *Did you say posterior?* and bends over.

Soul can't stop laughing: *You're such an ass*!

They decide to try this again when neither one is looking.

*

Self & Soul on Tour

In Paris, Self & Soul
fall in love

with each other—

sporting a witty beret.
eating bread and paté,

I can see it in your eyes, *oh*!
aren't we charming at the Deux Magots.

*

Who's on First?

Self & Soul are arguing about cause & effect,
whether the bird at the bird feeder
is the cause of the feeder or the effect,

                whether

one of them is the feeder while
the other is the bird and if the one who feeds
is also the one who feeds.

    *

The Value of the Liberal Arts

Self thinks Soul knows
if they're going to Heaven or Hell.

Soul thinks only Self can know.

Sometimes they wonder if
      Hell's actually Soul
            and Heaven's actually Self,

and then they remember Blake.

    *

Self 301

Staring out the window,
Self is trying to reflect
what it feels like
to stare out the window,
not as easy as it seems,
what with synapses snapping
and Soul barking orders.

*

Soul 301

Staring out the window,
Soul is trying
to clue Self in to focus on
the transparency of the glass
while congratulating themselves
on being able to focus
on the transparency of the glass.

IV.
Wander Window

Still Life, Nocturne in Shimmer and Bird

If I told you,
you who stick a finger in every eye,

if I told you, me sitting up in bed, the room opened
like a purse for the silver-coin moon,
that Christopher's sleeping plumbed the pull of tides,
and outside, there,
a bird at the bone-edge of the hour that is blue began to sing,
we lone two, its heart and my heart, awake, alive,
       wanting to speak of our power,

if I told you, for some reason even I don't understand,
that I began to cry, what would you believe?

Ubiquitous Porosities

Our bodies' ubiquitous porosities...
so often our bodies are the bodies of others
    —Ross Gay, *The Book of Delights*

Someone I don't know remembers me,
my picture stored in a psyche-file,
mind-drawer that opens now and then,
when they're 3am thought-cycling
and here's that jolt: *Oh, her again*,
kid whose coat got caught on a swing,
woman in the yellow dress,
girl sitting on her hands that day at the beach.

There was this woman on the Tube, reading Proust.
Perfect, aquiline nose, black curly hair pulled up,
away from her face. Small-boned, undeterred.
I can see her at will, as if she were a sister or friend,
as if part of me lingers in her image,
as if I didn't make the fact of her existence up at all.

Story

My teenaged, little sister, brokenhearted, crying,
some guy.

        This will happen

I told her: one day, you'll be in love and married. You'll move
to L.A. and have children, a boy and a girl.

Driving home from work, you'll think,
what was his name, that guy, was it Steve? Was it Scott?

"Tell me another story," she said,
sitting up, "one with rivers and seasons."

        A beginning.
        An end.

The stones marking my garden path, one and the next
and the next, know things I don't. But

that's only later, where I turn.
First, could be fire and rising seas.

Second, brutality and fear. Third, illness and great death.
Then the animals start talking,

which is always a sign.

In my dreams, in the parks, pure as bells,
they appear.

Something's going to happen,
something will be revealed

        once upon a time . . .

Frost, Midnight, the Burbs

A girl stares out her bedroom window
alone, at night, at the snow. The house is sleeping.
She's tucked her legs up under
her gown, encircled knees to chest. Something
seems like God. She thinks maybe, is that an owl?
Yes, a small one, like her. Yard, street, and town,
the entire world. Yard and street and town
heavy with life are dreams. Just now. Just here,
her sister in the upper bunk, her breathing knits
one-to-another stitches of thought,
outer-to-inner space
                          and the streetlight blazing
the snow omens a way of being
she can't foresee. In her little room,
her little skin, she knows only this icicle of time
frozen in mind. This moment, quietly shining,
this silence, will someday come back to call.

Though this is far away.

I'd like to tell her   what?
Everything. Something.
Nothing in the end.

Therefore, is she solitary.
Therefore, is she glad.

Sometimes the World Makes Itself Known to You

Heat like a hand over your mouth and nose. Heat
like old age. You're scrolling news, screen-eyed, on the porch:
who tweeted what/the latest must-read.

Sometimes you're in two places at once,
isn't that so?
both awake and asleep, in love and not. Sometimes,

your arm is touched so lightly, you barely notice.
But you do. Small as a child's, a finger of cool air
insists. Odd, isn't it? That change can be

imperceptible.
Birds now are talking to each other.
Nubile clouds have appeared, and you've turned
in a breath to see as the little earth asked.

From a Perception of Only 3 Senses or 3 Elements None Could Deduce a Fourth or Fifth

You too have wondered, half-minded,
if that mark on the bathroom floor is bug

or lint, has stirred, or is it
the quiver of your eye, blood pulsing through,

that lends its life?
In the garden, I couldn't decide: frog or rock?

In the dizzy half-light, shadow/sun,
stern, I settled on rock. Then frog for sure.

The brain, I'm told, jigsaws how eye sees,
piecing in gaps with what it expects is there.

Blake saw angels perched in a tree
and imaged in gold leaf the ghost of a flea.

I want to choose to believe in the good.

I Don't Know What I Mean by this Poem, but I Know It's True

An owl can hear a mouse's heart
                       below six feet of snow.

It's like this: at light fail, she quiets
               to the muffled thrum.

                    No wind.
No other rustle. The thrum under,

steady drum of breath/breaths, hers,
        who is alone, bounded by white,

and hers, alone, bounded by white
        as well.

              Sometimes, too:
your own heart hums

in the white noise of a small day,

like the scratch of tiny-boned feet,
the soft-chuck of a slow-winking eye.

Listen,
        it says, as you wait
        for the kill,

this is something, you know you know.

Those We Love

If, just now, looking up, I see my father or mother
outside the screen door, or any friend who's died,

if they stood in the framing light made by the open door,
I wouldn't be, somehow, surprised.

How right it is for them to be here. Sane as breath. Though I'd ask,
yes, where they'd been, were they fine, and there would be

something about moving away, something like that,
and I'd nod, and we'd have a coffee at the kitchen table.

In this greenworld light, dankish as a garden of ferns,
and outside, the air lifting children's voices at play

and in the honeysuckle, the tingle of birds.

Scientists Find New Organs in the Center of the Head

They appear to be a fourth pair of large salivary glands, tucked into the space where the nasal cavity meets the throat
—New York Times

Just behind the pharynx, above
        the torus tubarius, two glands
                that spit a quart of dribble each day

have lived like anchoresses for years, silently
        attending the tongue. No wonder
                my Pop-Tarts taste so heady, why

speech comes oiled for sport.
        These gals sure are wild
                or whoever put them up to it is,

but, mum's the word--
        I've got your back, you Thou-ness, as you have ours,
                the small, chaste muscle linking spine

to skull that gives us leave to jive,
        not to mention
                the Tahiti of the female pearl, secreted isle of joy.

Surely, some other monkish limb or bone
        awaits, yet to be revealed,
                an ear-like organ hiding athwart

the heart that frissons at human kindness or,
        lacing the lifeline of the palm, nerves retractable
                with push-button ease.

Clean the Glass, Open the Window

The corner
        I can't see around

is me, also the chair leg
        on which my toe stubs.

I'm holding my head
        underwater,

confounded by
        my own lack of breath.

                Okay, I get it:

Deconstruct
        to construct,

peel paper-thin skin,
        unwind tendons, veins,

unhinge bones,
        let air, at long last,

alleluia, Baby, through.

Kind of Thing that Happens When Nothing Happens

We were going somewhere
or coming back from somewhere.

We stopped for gas somewhere,
an off-the-highway town on a street

    I don't remember,
and me, I'm waiting for you to pay up,

come with coffee, maybe a Coke,
something like that. I forget.

    And yet,
I know I opened the car door for air,

dangling out one leg,
and the sky was Midwestern

blue & white, vast, vast, and this,
this climbed into the back for the ride.

Andromeda Galaxy in Ultraviolet

The word *package* arrived when I was six, the squeegee
sound of the last syllable like three Tootsie Rolls in the mouth, as if
    something
brown-boxed-unknown beyond the white kitchen and cereal and milk
of our flat had landed from outer space, a mysteriousness just for me.
Likewise, when I read "Andromeda Galaxy in Ultraviolet" headlining
an image of the heathery-lavendery-tanzanite swirl full of "hot, young,
    massive stars,"
I had to get up and walk around. I had to swear. "Holy Hell!"

Not for the photo, let's be clear, but for naked, dreamt of Andromeda,
    her name unchained
from the rocks, her name escaping into mist, into fire. For *galaxy*, as
    unthinkable, vast,
as the tiniest negative number funneling from zero down. And of
    ultraviolet? What can be said?
A violet somehow more than itself, the plumish, spring-born flower,
    Sappho's beloved,
navel-blossom adorned, a light blooming, light all around, a light
    way too light for us to see.

The Road was a Ribbon of Moonlight

> *The Highwayman*, Alfred Noyes

How does it happen, you think you're waiting
at an open window for love, listening in the dark,
for the faintest clip of heel or hoof. The world holds
its breath. But the trigger is just right there.
You can feel with your thumb its cold, true self. So
much is beautiful. It breaks us.
All poetry is about death,
I tell my students, and they, at first, demur,
not wanting to let that into their lives.
But *the moon is a ghostly galleon*, they cry.

Oh, I know. I know.

Acknowledgments

"Angel from Montgomery," *Autumn Sky Poetry Daily*

"My Sister and I Tease Each Other Over Which of Us Will Be More Wrecked by the Death of Our Spouses," *Barrow Street*

"Archeologists Discover Mummy with Golden Tongue," *EcoTheo*

"A House Once Experienced," *Fifthwednesday Journal*

"Kind of Thing that Happens When Nothing Happens," *Georgia Review*

"Story of a Little Time," "Over," *Indelible*

"Still of the Tongue," "Girls at Play Learn that Exquisite the Body," "The House Teaches Her About Death," "The House Teaches Her About Love," "The House Becomes Strange," *Live Encounters*

"Death of a Nine-Month-Old Girl, Not My Own," "All God's Creatures," *Menacing Hedge*

"Alternative Facts," *Michigan Quarterly Review*

"A Thing or Two About Illness," *Nimrod*

"Sometimes the World Makes Itself Known to You," *Painted Bride Quarterly*

"Soul 101," "Self 101," "Soul & Self," "This is Just," "Soul Needs Its Space," "What Self Learns from Soul," "What Soul Learns from Self," *Puerto del Sol*

"J.M.W. Turner, *Slavers Throwing overboard the Dead and Dying—Typhoon coming on*," *Rhino*

"Those We Love," *San Pedro River Review*

About the Author

Susan Azar Porterfield is the author of three previous books of poetry: *In the Garden of Our Spines*, *Kibbe* (Mayapple Press) and *Dirt, Root, Silk*, which won the Cider Press Review Editor's Prize. Individual poems are in *Michigan Quarterly Review*, *The Georgia Review*, *Barrow Street*, *EcoTheo*, *Painted Bride*, *Mid-American Review*, *North American Review*, *Crab Orchard Review*, *Nimrod*, *Rhino*, *Puerto del Sol*, *Poetry Ireland Review*, *Slipstream*, *Room*, *Ambit*, *Magma*. She is the editor of *Zen, Poetry, the Art of Lucien Stryk* (Ohio UP) and has written for *Poets & Writers*, *The Writer's Chronicle*, *Translation Review*, *The Midwest Journal of the Modern Language Association*. She is the recipient of an Illinois Arts Council Award for Poetry and a Fulbright to Lebanon. She has a Ph.D. in Literature and a M.A. in British Art from the Courtauld Institute in London.

About the Book

Voice / Poems was designed at Trio House Press through the collaboration of:

Heidi Czerwiec, Lead Editor
Lisa Ronan, Supporting Editor
Natasha Kane, Interior Designer
Jeffrey Scherer, Cover Artist
Baonhia Xiong, Cover Designer

The text is set in Adobe Caslon Pro.

About the Press

Trio House Press is an independent nonprofit press based in Minneapolis, Minnesota. We publish poetry and prose that moves, inspires, and encourages connection, empathy, and understanding, with a special emphasis on underrepresented voices and topics. To find out more about Trio House Press, please visit our website at http://www.triohousepress.org

www.ingramcontent.com/pod-product-compliance
Lightning Source LLC
Chambersburg PA
CBHW060539080526
44586CB00012B/795